# BARRON'S

# SAT®
# EXPRESS

D0035929

**Tim Hassall, M.A.**

**Dennis Hasson**

## BARRON'S

## Acknowledgments

Tim Hassall: I would like to thank Pete Mavrikis for his vision and help every step of the way and Annie Bernberg for her advice in the early stages of the book. Last, I thank my wife, Michele, and my sons, Daniel and Jack, for all their support.

Dennis Hasson: I would like to thank my wife, Marie Elena, and my twin daughters, Grace and Willow, for all their help and patience. I would also like to give a special thanks to my mathematics partner, Kevin Kozak. His hard work and guidance were remarkable.

## About the Authors

Tim Hassall is a partner for HASSSAT, a test preparation company in New Jersey. An English teacher, Tim is the author of three other books.

Dennis Hasson is a partner for HASSSAT, a test preparation company in New Jersey. Dennis is a 23-year mathematics teacher in Haddonfield, New Jersey.

*All inquiries should be addressed to:*
Barron's Educational Series, Inc.
250 Wireless Boulevard
Hauppauge, NY 11788
**www.barronseduc.com**

ISBN: 978-1-4380-0990-2
Library of Congress Control Number: 2017930250

Printed in Canada
9 8 7 6 5 4 3 2 1

**10%**
**POST-CONSUMER WASTE**
Paper contains a minimum of 10% post-consumer waste (PCW). Paper used in this book was derived from certified, sustainable forestlands.